W9-BZT-933

CELESTIAL MANDALAS

COLORING BOOK

MARTY NOBLE

DOVER PUBLICATIONS, INC.
MINEOLA, NEW YORK

From the Sun and Moon to an array of planets, stars, clouds, and charming figures, these designs inspired by the endless wonders of the sky are incorporated into a variety of pleasingly symmetrical mandalas. Full of graceful patterns and shapes, each coloring page evokes celestial beauty. A unique opportunity for the experienced colorist, more than thirty illustrations provide limitless possibilities for experimentation. Plus, the perforated pages make displaying your work easy!

Copyright

Copyright © 2016 by Dover Publications, Inc.
All rights reserved.

Bibliographical Note

Celestial Mandalas Coloring Book is a new work,
first published by Dover Publications, Inc., in 2016.

International Standard Book Number

ISBN-13: 978-0-486-80480-4
ISBN-10: 0-486-80480-1

Manufactured in the United States by RR Donnelley
80480102   2016
www.doverpublications.com